MARY QUEEN of SCOTS

an anthology of poetry
chosen and with an introduction by

ANTONIA FRASER

illustrated by Rebecca Fraser

Eyre Methuen, London   The Greville Press

First published in 1981 jointly
by Eyre Methuen Ltd
11 New Fetter Lane, London EC4P 4EE
and the Greville Press
Emscote Lawn, Warwick

British Library Cataloguing in Publication data:

Mary Queen of Scots: an anthology of poetry.
1. Poetry, modern — Translations into English
2. English poetry — Translations from foreign literature
I. Fraser, Antonia
808.81'9'351   PN6110.M27/

ISBN 0-413-48550-1

Printed in Great Britain
by BAS Printers Ltd, Over Wallop, Stockbridge

Mary Queen of Scots
Poetry Anthology

" Wauken be nicht and broden on some
bune,
Glamour of saul or spiritual grace,
I have seen sancts an angels iy her
face
    And, like a frere of seraphy, me mune."
               Lewis Spence.

With all best wishes for
Christmass 1989
         Douglas

This book was formerly included in
 the personal library of **Miss Meta Wright**,
former English teacher at Dornoch Academy.
She graciously bequeathed her library to the
school on the condition that it was upgraded.

For Flora and Robert – an Epithalamium
29 March 1980

Contents

Acknowledgements

For permission to reprint copyright material, the following acknowledgements are made:

Caroline Bingham: reprinted by permission of the author and Weidenfeld and Nicolson Ltd, from *The Kings and Queens of Scotland*; D. B. Wyndham Lewis: reprinted by permission of Sheed and Ward Ltd from *Ronsard*; Stephen Spender: reprinted by permission of Faber and Faber Ltd, from Schiller's *Mary Stuart*; Marion Angus: reprinted by permission of Faber and Faber Ltd, from *The Turn of the Day*; Alfred Noyes: reprinted by permission of William Blackwood and Sons, from *Tales of the Mermaid Tavern*; Edith Sitwell: reprinted by permission of David Higham Associates Ltd, from *Collected Poems* published by Macmillan and Co. Ltd; Michael Harari: reprinted by permission of the author and William Collins Sons & Co. Ltd, from Boris Pasternak's *Poems 1955–59*; Iain Crichton Smith: reprinted by permission of the author and Eyre and Spottiswoode, from *Thistles and Roses*.

Editor's note

The idea for this book was suggested to me by Anthony Astbury of Greville Press, who shares my passion for its subject, I am greatly indebted to him, and the G. H. Godbert, also of Greville Press, not only for the inspiration but also for their enthusiasm throughout. Amongst others, I am particularly grateful to Sally Purcell for noble research; and to John Heath-Stubbs who made suggestions, including the poem 'Chastelard to Mary Stuart' by Eugene Lee-Hamilton.

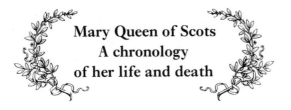

Mary Queen of Scots
A chronology
of her life and death

1542

8 December Mary is born at the Palace of Linlithgow to James V and Mary of Guise.

14 December She becomes Queen of Scotland on the death of her father.

1548

Mary is betrothed to François, Dauphin of France, son of Henri II, and sails to France where she lives with her mother's relatives, the powerful Guise family.

1558

24 April The marriage of Mary and François.

17 November Death of Mary Tudor, Queen of England. The English throne is claimed for Mary Stuart by her father-in-law on the grounds that Elizabeth is, by Catholic standards, illegitimate.

1559

10 July Death of Henri II; François succeeds to the French throne.

1560

5 December François II dies.

1561

Mary returns to Scotland, arriving at Leith in August. Despite her own commitment to Catholicism, she pursues a policy of religious toleration towards her Protestant subjects.

1562

Mary creates her Protestant half-brother, Lord James Stewart, the Earl of Moray as a reward for suppressing an insurrection by the leading Catholic magnate, the Earl of Huntly.

1565

Mary marries her cousin, Henry, Lord Darnley, son of the Earl of Lennox. Like Mary herself, he can claim to be Elizabeth's successor. The marriage antagonizes Elizabeth and also angers Moray who, resenting his own loss of influence over his half-sister, raises an abortive rebellion against her and then flees to England.

1566

Deterioration of Mary's relations with Darnley, who demands the Crown Matrimonial and becomes the focus for the Protestant opposition to Mary.

9 March The murder, in Mary's presence (while she is six months pregnant), of David Riccio, her Italian secretary, whom Darnley falsely suspects of being her lover. Darnley deserts his Protestant allies and flees with Mary to Dunbar. The Protestant opposition temporarily collapses.

19 June Mary gives birth to a son, James. As Mary's estrangement from Darnley deepens, she turns increasingly to James Hepburn, Earl of Bothwell.

October Mary falls seriously ill at Jedburgh, following a visit to Bothwell at the military outpost of Hermitage Castle.

December James is christened at Stirling Castle. Darnley does not attend the ceremony.

1567

January Darnley falls ill; Mary accompanies him from Glasgow, a centre of Lennox power, to Edinburgh where his support is slender.

10 February Murder of Darnley at Kirk o'Field, probably by Bothwell and his associates, and members of the Douglas family.

April Bothwell is acquitted of Darnley's murder by a Parliament intimidated by the number of his armed adherents in Edinburgh.

19 April The Ainslie Bond, in which Bothwell suggests he should marry Mary, is signed by a group of Scots noblemen.

23 April Bothwell abducts Mary as she returns to Edinburgh after visiting her baby son at Stirling and takes her to Dumbarton Castle.

1 May Bothwell's enemies meet at Stirling and sign another bond, swearing to remove Mary from Bothwell's influence. The signatories include Morton, Argyll and Atholl, who only ten days before had signed the Ainslie Bond.

15 May Mary marries Bothwell at Holyrood Palace in a Protestant ceremony.

15 June Bothwell's enemies, the 'confederate lords', and the royal army confront each other at Carberry Hill. Mary refuses to abandon Bothwell but as her army deserts her, she agrees to accept a safe-conduct for him and to surrender herself to the rebels. Bothwell flees while Mary finds herself abused as an adulteress and the bride of her husband's murderer. She is taken to Edinburgh but is lodged not at the Castle or Holyrood Palace but in the house of the Laird of Craigmillar, where she collapses in despair.

16 June Mary is imprisoned in Lochleven Castle.

c. 19–24 July Mary miscarries of twins. She is forced to abdicate in favour of her son James and a regency government is to be established under Moray.

December Mary is publicly blamed before Parliament for the murder of Darnley. The first mention of the so-called Casket Letters incriminating her.

1568
May Mary escapes from Lochleven with the aid of a young page, Willie Douglas. She rapidly gathers an army but is defeated by Moray's forces at Langside.

16 May Mary flees to England and appeals to Elizabeth for help. She is denied access to the English court and is moved to the isolated castle of Bolton in Yorkshire.

October 'The Conference of York' opens to try Mary of complicity in Darnley's murder. Moray attends and produces the 'Casket Letters' as evidence against her. Mary is not permitted to appear in person or to inspect the 'Letters' (which were never at any point shown to her).

1569
January The conference concludes with no firm verdict but Moray returns to Scotland while Mary remains a prisoner under the charge of the Earl of Shrewsbury, who is

to be her gaoler for the next fifteen years.

Mary becomes the rallying point for a long series of Catholic plots against Elizabeth. Conspiracy to marry Mary to the Duke of Norfolk, the leading English Catholic.

1570

Promulgation of Papul Bull excommunicating Elizabeth and releasing her Catholic subjects from their loyalty to her.

August Ridolfi Plot to place Mary and Norfolk on the throne with the aid of Spanish troops.

1572

Execution of Norfolk for treason. Elizabeth resists pressure to execute Mary as well.

1581

Mary proposes an Association between herself and James whereby they should rule Scotland jointly. James betrays her and indicates to Elizabeth that he has no desire for his mother to be released.

1583

Throckmorton Plot, inspired by Mary's Guise relatives, is uncovered by Francis Walsingham, Elizabeth's Secretary of State.

1585

Sir Amyas Paulet succeeds Shrewsbury as Mary's gaoler and transforms her imprisonment into the strictest possible confinement.

Act of Association passed by the English Parliament condemning to death not only anyone plotting against Queen Elizabeth but also anyone in whose favour such plots are instigated.

1586

The Babington Plot, a conspiracy by a group of young English Catholics to place Mary on the throne, is uncovered by Walsingham who also produces sufficient proof of Mary's complicity to convince Elizabeth of her cousin's guilt.

September The Babington Conspirators are tried and executed.

15 October Trial of Mary Queen of Scots opens at Fotheringhay Castle.

25 October Mary is found guilty of 'compassing and imagining . . . matters relating to the death and destruction of the Queen of England'.

1587

1 February Elizabeth signs Mary's death warrant.

8 February Execution of Mary at Fotheringhay.

July Mary is buried in Peterborough Cathedral.

1612

Mary's body is moved to Westminster Abbey where it lies in a tomb built by her son, James VI and I.

Introduction

Poets have always felt the enchantment of Mary Queen of Scots: Burns and Wordsworth, Swinburne and Pasternak. In her own lifetime she first cast the spell. 'Above all,' wrote Brantôme, 'she delighted in poetry and poets . . . I have often seen her read to herself in France and Scotland, with tears in her eyes and sighs in her heart.'

This passion was reciprocated. The poets, led by Ronsard, paid their hommage. Ronsard, the most prominent member of the Pléiade group, knew the graceful girl Dauphiness of the French court well (they had in common a knowledge of the harsher land of Scotland where Ronsard had been in attendance on Mary's father) and it has been suggested that he published the first collected edition of his works in 1560 in response to Mary's request. Certainly he kept her portrait continually in front of him in his library. To Ronsard Mary in the flush of youth was '*o belle et plus que belle et agréable Aurore*'; and of the sad captive nearly twenty years later he wrote (in Jonathan Griffin's translation):

> Your eye, which has no rival in the world
> Is never banished from my heart by time . . .

Although Maisonfleur's odes to Mary have not survived, to another member of the Pléiade, Joachim du Bellay, who celebrated her in several sonnets, she was Astraea; with her 'royal honour and royal grace' Mary was destined to usher in an age of gold.

One poet indeed died for the love of Mary Queen of Scots. Pierre de Châstelard accompanied her back to Scotland as a page, and on their journey, he declared, the galleys needed no lanterns to light their way 'since the eyes of this Queen suffice to light up the whole sea with their lovely fire'. The tragic end to his story remains to speak almost as cogently as verse of her powerful attraction: on the eve of his execution – for prosecuting his mad passion beyond all limits – Châstelard called Mary 'the most beautiful and the most cruel princess in the world'.

Mary's own verses are of a modest nature – an expression of grief on the death of her young husband, exclamations of despair at a burdensome imprisonment; but poetry itself was in her blood. We do not have to look back as far as her fifteenth-century ancestor, James I of Scotland, author of the long and poignant poem written to Lady Joan Beaufort, *The Kingis Quhair*. We have the word of Sir David Lindsay of the Mount, the poet and satirist, that Mary's own father James V wrote verses.

Mary's second husband – and cousin – the glamorous but unworthy Lord Darnley, wrote charming love poems in the courtly tradition, in one of which he described Mary as 'the well of womanhood'. (The only child of their ill-fated union, James VI and I, would incidentally also prove a considerable poet: one whose works are regrettably underestimated today.) Poetry then, and song, never to be totally distinguished from poetry, at least in Scotland, was natural to the air breathed by this Renaissance princess, described by a contemporary as 'personally the most beautiful in Europe'.

And since Mary's death the lyrics have not ceased to crown her. It is not surprising that this should be so. After all one may fairly claim for Mary Queen of Scots that she is the most romantic heroine in history. Who can challenge her? Helen perhaps – but she is mythical, a mere flutter of robes causing the old men to raise their eyes as she walked along the walls of Troy. When Ronsard wrote of Mary the young widow, pacing sadly in her white mourning at Fontainebleau, her garments blowing about her as she walked, like the sails of a ship ruffled in the wind, he described reality. Besides, Helen's story had a happy ending – at least for Helen. Mary Queen of Scots lived: and thanks to poets, playwrights, composers and film makers (not forgetting historians) lives on. Her tragic end has seen to that. In the words of Pasternak, translated by Michael Harari:

> Her death's heroic; this keeps her at her prime
> Traps her in rumour; she's the talk of time.

Nevertheless it is significant that the many poems written to and about this romantic heroine are by no means uniform in their approval of her conduct, nor for that matter uniform in their attitude to her dramatic destiny. In this respect the poets do not, as one might have expected, divide from the historians.

The historiography of Mary Queen of Scots is a highly complex subject: already long before her death, propagandists were at work in slanting her story towards their particular angle. However, one can summarize it to the extent of saying that historians have seen her in four principal roles. First there is Mary as the Dynastic Rival to Queen Elizabeth I (a view taken in the main by English historians) who wrongfully claimed her throne on the grounds of Elizabeth's supposed illegitimacy. The opposing – mainly Catholic – point of view sees Mary as the Martyr Queen, cruelly cut down by her Protestant cousin in a religious cause. Third, there is Mary the Scarlet Woman, that is, the adulterous lover of Bothwell, author of the Casket Letters and murderess of Darnley. Fourth, there is the concept of Mary as a *femme fatale*, helplessly alluring, not responsible for those disasters which attended her, a patient of history not its agent.

It is fascinating to discover all these various historians'

notions of Mary's character also at work in the poets' consciousness. Let us take Mary as the Dynastic Rival: nothing haunted her politically so much as the ill-judged pretension made on her behalf by her father-in-law Henri II of France to the English throne, on the grounds that Henry VIII's marriage to Anne Boleyn was unrecognized by the Catholic Church and Elizabeth, their offspring, was thus a bastard. In Mary's lifetime du Bellay referred to 'the three great peoples subject to you' – England, as well as Scotland and France, a line which would have infuriated Queen Elizabeth. (But perhaps the nineteenth-century child Marjory Fleming put matters in perspective when she wrote firmly, in lines included here: 'Elisbeth was a cross old maid'.)

Schiller's great play *Maria Stuart* centres round a meeting of the two Queens, Elizabeth and Mary, the latter by now the captive of the former. It is true that this fabulous meeting never actually took place, but the licence not permitted to historians must be allowed to poets. Mary, provoked beyond endurance, bursts out:

> England is
> Ruled by a bastard, and a noble people
> Corrupted by a cunning trickster . . .

Here Schiller, quoted in Stephen Spender's translation, brilliantly incarnates the dynastic issue. It is a moment equally unforgettable in Donizetti's opera *Maria Stuarda*, based on Schiller's play, when Maria cries out: '*Vil bastarda* . . . .'

The most beautiful of all the poems to the Martyr Queen, 'Decease, Release,' was written by the English Jesuit Robert Southwell shortly after Mary's execution. Its line, 'Alive a Queen, now dead I am a Saint' proved an accurate prophecy. As for Mary the Scarlet Woman, Iain Crichton Smith, writing in Scotland today, gives us still the vengeful voice of John Knox:

> A thunderous God tolls from a northern sky.
> He pulls the clouds like bandages awry.
> See how the harlot bleeds below her crown . . .
> The shearing naked absolute blade has torn
> Through false French roses to her foreign cry.

This is Mary 'the White Rose-tree', in Edith Sitwell's phrase, contrasted with Knox, 'the bitter Man of Thorns'.

Lastly, the *femme fatale* has bewitched the poets down history and aroused their chivalry: for it is in the distant exotic world of chivalry, here captured by Rebecca Fraser's illustrations, that Mary in one sense lives forever. James Hogg's 'Song' from *The Queen's Wake* is redolent of doomed beauty:

> Though courtiers fawned and ladies sung,
> Still in her ear the accents rung, –
> *'Watch thy young bosom, and maiden eye,*
> *For the shower must fall and the flowret die.'*

My own secret favourite, 'Alas! Poor Queen' by Marion Angus, belongs to the *femme fatale* category, but it is the human face of the enchantress.

> Queens should be cold and wise,
> And she loved little things,
> > Parrots
> > And red-legged partridges
> And the golden fishes of the Duc de Guise
> And the pigeon with the blue ruff
> She had from Monsieur d'Elbœuf.

This is the Mary who radiated something more than mere surface charm and beauty: in addition she possessed a kind of winning intimacy. We find it in her own letters, as well as the inventories and accounts which bring her alive down four centuries: it is the combination which dazzles.

Finally it was Mary herself who made the most appropriate summation of her fortunes when she chose as her motto: 'In my end is my beginning'. Certainly the poets will never let her go.

ANTONIA FRASER

Mary Queen of Scots
Poetry Anthology

The Absent One

Wherever I may be
In the woods or in the fields
Whatever the hour of day
Be it dawn or the eventide
My heart still feels it yet
The eternal regret.

As I sink into my sleep
The absent one is near
Alone upon my couch
I feel his beloved touch
In work or in repose
We are forever close.

MARY QUEEN OF SCOTS [1542–87]
Translated by Antonia Fraser

*Celebration of the wedding of Mary and the Dauphin,
24 April 1558, at the Palace of the Parliament, Paris*

from The Kings and Queens of Scotland

One thought maintains my hours of solitude,
Yet sweet and bitter grows my mood in turn;
Doubt freezes me, and then with hope I burn,
Till sleep and rest my aching heart elude.
Dear sister, see how I lack quietude:
Desire to meet with you oppresses me;
The torment of delay distresses me.
Let my words end this long incertitude!
I've seen a ship blown wildly from her course,
In sight of port, but 'ere she came to land
Driven again into the raging sea.
Likewise I fear to come to grief perforce.
Oh, do not think I fear it at your hand!
But Fate can mar the fairest destiny.

MARY QUEEN OF SCOTS [1542–87]
Translated by Caroline Bingham

from The Kings and Queens of Scotland

What am I, alas, what purpose has my life?
I nothing am, a corpse without a heart,
A useless shade, a victim of sad strife,
One who lives yet, and wishes to depart.
My enemies, no envy hold for me;
My spirit has no taste for greatness now.
Sorrow consumes me in extreme degree,
Your hatred shall be satisfied, I vow.
And you, my friends, you who have held me dear,
Reflect that I, lacking both health and fortune,
Cannot aspire to any great deed here.
Welcome, therefore, my ultimate misfortune.
And pray that when affliction ends my story,
Then I may have some share in Heaven's glory.

MARY QUEEN OF SCOTS [1542–87]
Translated by Caroline Bingham

Spoken by a Diamond

Adamas in cordis effigiem sculptus, annulogue insertus,
quem Maria Scotorum Regina ad Elizabetham Anglorum
Reginam misit anno M.D. LXIV.

It is not my substance makes me proud,
that neither fire nor iron can harm,
nor my unstained brilliance, nor my
pure light's clarity, nor the craftsman's skill
that gave me this form, and elegantly
clothed me round with eloquent gold:
but because I express my Mistress' heart
so clearly, that eyes could not see it
more plainly if they saw it in her body.
Thus each heart has unmoved constancy,
unstained brilliance, and pure
light's clarity, hiding no guile within:
equal in all but hardness.
Secondly Fate is kind to me,
in letting me hope to see
such a Heroine as I never hoped for
after having left my Mistress.
May Fate grant I link *their* two hearts
in adamantine bonds,
never to be loosed by jealousy, suspicion,
envy, hate, or advancing years;
then I should be happiest of gems,
as I am clearest,
as I am dearest,
as I am hardest of gems.

GEORGE BUCHANAN [1506–82]
Translated by Sally Purcell

Marriage of Darnley and Mary at Holyrood, 29 July 1565

To the Queen of Scotland

Not without purpose did Heaven set in you
Beauties of spirit and beauty of face,
So much royal honour and royal grace,
And even more is promised as your due.

Not without purpose have Fates that hold true,
To allot the pride of Spain a lower place,
By right of allies or by right of race
Decreed three great peoples subject to you.

They wish that through you France and England may
    transform
To a long peace the hereditary war
Which from father to son has so long rolled.

They wish that through you the fair maid Astraea
May in this iron age once more appear
And we once more see the fair Age of Gold.

JOACHIM DU BELLAY [1522–61]
Translated by Jonathan Griffin

Though now the sea holds us far apart,
The brightness of your lovely sun,
Your eye, which has no rival in the world,
Is never banished from my heart by time . . . .
Queen, you who imprison a Queen so rare,
Soften your wrath and change your mind,
The sun from its rising to its sinking to sleep
Views no more barbarous act on this earth!
People, your degenerate lack of will to fight
Shames your forebears, Renauld, Lancelot, and Roland,
Who with glad hearts took up ladies' wrongs
And guarded them, and rescued them—where you,
    Frenchmen,
Have not dared to look at or to touch your arms,
To save from slavery such a lovely Queen!

PIERRE DE RONSARD [1524–85]
Translated by Dominic Wyndham Lewis

Earl Bothwell Ballad

This ballad represents the murder of Darnley as done in revenge for his complicity in the murder of Riccio. The Regent Moray is described as 'banishing' Queen Mary, whereupon she fled to England. Mary escaped from Lochleven Castle on 2 May 1568 and took refuge in England on the sixteenth. We must suppose the ballad to have been made not long after.

1 Woe worth thee, woe worth thee, false Scottlande!
    Ffor thou hast euer wrought by a sleight;
  For the worthyest prince that euer was borne,
    You hanged under a cloud by night.

2 The Queene of France a letter wrote,
    And sealed itt with hart and ringe,
  And bade him come Scottland within,
    And shee wold marry him and crowne him king.

3 To be a king, itt is a pleasant thing,
    To bee a prince vnto a peere;
  But you haue heard, and so haue I too,
    A man may well by gold to deere.

4 There was an Italyan in that place,
    Was as wel beloued as euer was hee;
  Lord David was his name,
    Chamberlaine vnto the queene was hee.

5 Ffor if the king had risen forth of his place,
    He wold haue sitt him downe in the cheare,
  And thos itt beseemed him not soe well,
    Altho the king had beene present there.

6 Some lords in Scottland waxed wonderous wroth,
    And quarrelld with him for the nonce;
  I shall you tell how itt beffell;
    Twelve daggers were in him all att once.

7 When this queene see the chamberlaine was slaine,
    For him her cheeks shee did weete,
  And made a vow for a twelue month and a day
    The king and shee wold not come in one sheete.

8 Then some of the lords of Scottland waxed wrothe,
    And made their vow vehementlye,
  'For death of the queenes chamberlaine
    The king himselfe he shall dye.'

9 They strowed his chamber ouer with gunpowder,
    And layd greene rushes in his way;
  Ffor the traitors thought that night
    The worthy king for to betray.

The murder of David Riccio, 9 March 1566, at Holyrood

10 To bedd the worthy king made him bowne,
　　To take his rest, that was his desire;
　He was noe sooner cast on sleepe,
　　But his chamber was on a blasing fyer.

11 Vp he lope, and a glasse window broke,
　　He had thirty foote for to ffall;
　Lord Bodwell kept a priuy wach
　　Vnderneath his castle-wall:
　'Who haue wee heere?' sayd Lord Bodwell;
　'Answer me, now I doe call.'

12 'King Henery the Eighth my vnekle was;
　　Some pitty show for his sweet sake!
　Ah, Lord Bodwell, I know thee well;
　　Some pitty on me I pray thee take!'

13 'I'le pitty thee as much', he sayd,
　　'And as much favor I'le show to thee
　As thou had on the queene's chamberlaine
　　That day thou deemedst him to dye.'

14 Through halls and towers this king they ledd,
　　Through castles and towers that were hye,
　Through an arbor into an orchard,
　　And there hanged him in a peare tree.

15 When the gouernor of Scottland he heard tell
    That the worthye king he was slaine,
  He hath banished the queene soe biterlye
    That in Scottland shee dare not remaine.

16 But shee is ffled into merry England,
    And Scottland to a side hath laine,
  And through the Queene of Englands good grace
    Now in England shee doth remaine.

ANONYMOUS

‿ 37 ‿

If Langour Makis Men Licht

If langour makis men licht,
Or dolour thame decoir,
In erth thair is no wicht
May me compair in gloir.
If cairfull thochtis restoir
My havy hairt frome sorrow,
I am for evermoir
In joy both evin and morrow.

If plesour be to pance,
I playnt me nocht opprest;
Or absence micht avance,
My hairt is haill possest.
If want of quiet rest
From cairis micht me convoy,
My mind is nocht mollest,
Bot evermoir in joy.

Thocht that I pance in pane
In passing to and fro,
I laubor all in vane;
For so hes mony mo
That hes nocht servit so
In suting of thair sueit.
The nar the fyre I go,
The grittar is my heit.

The turtour for hir maik
Mair dule may nocht indure
Nor I do for hir saik,
Evin hir wha hes in cure
My hart, whilk sal be sure
In service to the deid
Unto that lady pure,
The well of womanheid.

Schaw schedull to that sueit,
My pairt so permanent,
That no mirth whill we meit
Sall cause me be content;
Bot still my hairt lament
In sorrowfull siching soir
Till tyme scho be present.
Fairweill. I say no moir.

HENRY STUART, LORD DARNLEY [1545–67]

decoir *adorn*　　　　maik *mate*
gloir *glory*　　　　　dule *sorrow*
pance *think*　　　　schedull *statement*
turtour *turtle dove*　whill *until*

Decease Release
Dum morior orior

The pounded spice both tast and sent doth please,
In fading smoke the force doth incense shewe,
The perisht kernell springeth with encrease,
The lopped tree doth best and soonest growe.

Gods spice I was and pounding was my due,
In fadinge breath my incense savored best,
Death was the meane my kyrnell to renewe,
By loppinge shott I upp to heavenly rest.

Some thinges more perfect are in their decaye,
Like sparke that going out gives clerest light,
Such was my happ whose dolefull dying daye
Beganne my joy and termed fortunes spite.

Alive a Queene, now dead I am a Sainte,
Once N: calld, my name nowe Martyr is,
From earthly raigne debarred by restraint,
In liew whereof I raigne in heavenly blisse.

The royal entourage at Kirk o' Field, February 1567

My life my griefe, my death hath wrought my joye,
My frendes my foyle, my foes my weale procur'd,
My speedy death hath shortened longe annoye,
And losse of life an endles life assur'd.

My skaffold was the bedd where ease I founde,
The blocke a pillowe of Eternall reste,
My hedman cast me in a blisfull swounde,
His axe cutt off my cares from combred breste.

Rue not my death, rejoyce at my repose,
It was no death to me but to my woe,
The budd was opened to lett out the Rose,
The cheynes unloo'sd to lett the captive goe.

A prince by birth, a prisoner by mishappe,
From Crowne to crosse, from throne to thrall I fell,
My right my ruthe, my titles wrought my trapp,
My weale my woe, my worldly heaven my hell.

By death from prisoner to a prince enhaunc'd,
From Crosse to Crowne, from thrall to throne againe,
My ruth my right, my trapp my stile advaunc'd,
From woe to weale, from hell to heavenly raigne.

ROBERT SOUTHWELL [1561–95]

from **Corona Trágica**

In prison:

> While MARY'S life from day to day was passing
> At this time, another life she was living
> So saintly as to perfection be nearing,
> To the summit of which she was aspiring.
> Time that remained (if any was remaining)
> To friends and family she'd spend in writing
> A few letters, dignified, treasures to hold,
> Like Parian marble, and inscribed in gold.

From her last speech:

> I die happy because my tormented soul
> Arrives at the haven of eternal peace,
> So free from the blame of causing her offence
> That I have no need to speak in my defence.
>
> If I wished my body to be transported
> To France, it was so that there it might have found
> That which in England would not be provided,
> Catholic rites upon consecrated ground:
> And if this by your Queen should be prevented
> (Her breast encloses a hardness so profound)
> I pray God He may never separate her
> From the help of His church in any quarter.

She binds her eyes:

> MARY covers over the resplendent light
> Of each of her spheres (Love's own Green
>   Firmament),
> And if death were to behold your stars so bright
> Who'd ever think to kill you was his intent?

LOPE DE VEGA [1562–1635]
Translated by Bill Affleck

from **L'Escossoise**

Mary:

But though death to the wicked is a curse,
It's blessing to the good, whom the years' course
Guides to that port whose entry without pity
Threads the elect into the heavenly city—
Living, not dead, not old, young, they arise
Vagrant pilgrims made natives of the Skies.

So I having now run my race of years,
Borne constantly storm on storm's pains and fears
Through all my time afloat in the world tempest,
Would anchor in the harbour of all rest.

ANTOINE DE MONTCHRESTIEN [1575–1621]
Translated by Jonathan Griffin

Bothwell and Mary Queen of Scots, 1567

from **Maria Stuarda**

Mary to her father-in-law

Rizzio to me was a faithful adviser,
A shrewd judge of men, and secretary of skill;
Through him I stood safe amid party strife,
Through him each treacherous ambush
Of my insatiable bitter enemy
Elizabeth was foiled; through him, Lord Darnley
Won my hand—and with it my sceptre.
He did not disdain the low-born stranger then,
Not till by that stranger's means
He saw the crown. He grasped it: and what thanks
Did he give Rizzio? In the silent
Shades of night, beneath my royal roof,
Secure in hospitality, among unarmed ladies,
In front of me (already bearing
In my body the first pledge of once-dear love)
He came to his betrayal;
And with that low-born, as innocent, blood
He dared to befoul my table, my land,
My garments, my face, and my fame.

VITTORIO ALFIERI [1749–1803]
Translated by Sally Purcell

from **Maria Stuart**, Act I

Burleigh: It is, moreover, known that you have schemed
To overthrow the religion of this country
And to unite
All the Kings of Europe against England.

Mary: And if I have—I have not—but
Supposing that I had? I came here
A fugitive, entreating hospitality
From her, who is a Queen of my own blood.
Pleading for refuge, I was seized by force,
Begging a home, was cast into a prison.
I am held here against my right.
Is then my conscience answerable
To England? Is it not my duty, rather,
To call all monarchs—in the name of freedom
Protect and save me, answer force with force!
Yes, for there is no justice, only force,
In question between me and England.

Burleigh: Do not invoke the dreadful rights of force,
Lady. They do not favour prisoners.

Mary: I know it! I am weak, and she is strong.
Let her use force then, let her kill me,
Build on my sacrifice her safety—
But let her then confess that she employs
Force, only force.
When she would rid herself of her feared enemy,
The scabbard out of which she draws the sword
Is force, only force.
Tricks such as these will not deceive a world.
Let her dare show herself before
The world, for what she is!
Murder me, she may, she cannot judge me.

. . .

from **Act 3**

Elizabeth: Have you abandoned plotting? Is no murder
    In preparation? Will no adventurer
    Stake all to be the sad knight of your cause?
    —Yes, all is over, Lady Stuart. You no longer
    Persecute me. And the world has other cares.
    No one at this instant lusts to be
    Your fourth husband, for you kill your rescuers
    As you killed husbands.

Mary: Sister! Sister!
    Oh God, grant me patience.

Elizabeth: My Lord of Leicester, look now on the charms
    Of her no man could gaze upon unscathed.
    Well, well, your fame was won quite cheaply.
    To gain the general favour cost you nothing,
    You chose to make your favours general.

Mary: Oh—

Elizabeth: Look, look, Leicester, now she shows
    Her true face as it is. Till now we've seen
    Only the mask.

Mary: I was guilty in my youth of many follies
    When in my weakness I let strength seduce me
    But with a royal open-mindedness
    I did not hide my sinful deeds behind
    The false show of a virtuous-seeming face.
    The world knows what was worst in me, and I
    Am better, then, I think, than the world knows.

The abortive 'battle' of Carberry Hill, 15 June 1567

But you, alas for you, when futures will
Tear off the unctuous superfice that hides
The hot equator of your stolen lusts.
You cannot be said to have inherited
Virtue from your mother. We know what vices
Caused Anne Boleyn to mount the scaffold.

Talbot: Oh merciful God! That it should come to this!
Is this your self-control, your patience,
Lady Mary?

Mary: Patience! Self-control!
I have borne what is tolerable. Now let
My indignation so long sepulchred,
Spring from its grave! And you,
Who could teach to the basilisk
Its murderous glance, let my tongue learn from you
To dart forth venom!

Talbot: She is beside herself!
Ignore this madness!
(Elizabeth, speechless with rage, stares at Mary)

Mary: England is
Ruled by a bastard, and a noble people
Corrupted by a cunning trickster!
If there were justice, it is she
Who'd kneel to me, and I'd stand where she is!

(Exit Elizabeth and Followers)

FRIEDRICH SCHILLER [1759–1805]
Translated by Stephen Spender

Lament of
Mary Queen of Scots
on the Approach of Spring

Now Nature hangs her mantle green
    On every blooming tree,
And spreads her sheets o' daisies white
    Out o'er the grassy lea:
Now Phœbus chears the crystal streams,
    And glads the azure skies;
But nought can glad the weary wight
    That fast in durance lies.

Now laverocks wake the merry morn,
    Aloft on dewy wing;
The merle, in his noontide bower,
    Makes woodland echoes ring;
The mavis mild wi' many a note,
    Sings drowsy day to rest:
In love and freedom they rejoice,
    Wi' care nor thrall opprest.

Now blooms the lily by the bank,
    The primrose down the brae;
The hawthorn's budding in the glen,
    And milk-white is the slae:
The meanest hind in fair Scotland
    May rove their sweets amang;
But I, the Queen of a' Scotland,
    Maun lie in prison strang.

Mary at the house of the Laird of Craigmillar,
the Provost of Edinburgh, after Carberry Hill, June 1567

I was the Queen o' bonie France,
  Where happy I hae been;
Fu' lightly rase I on the morn,
  As blythe lay down at e'en:
And I'm the sovereign of Scotland,
  And mony a traitor there;
Yet here I lie in foreign bands,
  And never ending care.

But as for thee, thou false woman,
  My sister and my fae,
Grim vengeance, yet, shall whet a sword
  That thro' thy soul shall gae:
The weeping blood in woman's breast
  Was never known to thee;
Nor th' balm that draps on wounds of woe
  Frae woman's pitying e'e.

My son! my son! may kinder stars
  Upon thy fortune shine!
And may those pleasures gild thy reign,
  That ne'er wad blink on mine!
God keep thee frae thy mother's faes,
  Or turn their hearts to thee:
And where thou meet'st thy mother's friend,
  Remember him for me!

O! soon, to me, may summer-suns
    Nae mair light up the morn!
Nae mair, to me, the autumn winds
    Wave o'er the yellow corn!
And in the narrow house o' death
    Let winter round me rave;
And the next flowers, that deck the spring,
    Bloom on my peaceful grave.

ROBERT BURNS [1759–96]

Lament of Mary Queen of Scots
on the Eve of a New Year

I

Smile of the Moon!—for so I name
That silent greeting from above;
A gentle flash of light that came
From her whom drooping captives love;
Or art thou of still higher birth?
Thou that didst part the clouds of earth
My torpor to reprove!

II

Bright boon of pitying Heaven!—alas,
I may not trust thy placid cheer!
Pondering that Time to-night will pass
The threshold of another year;
For years to me are sad and dull;
My very moments are too full
Of hopelessness and fear.

III

And yet the soul-awakening gleam,
That struck perchance the farthest cone
Of Scotland's rocky wilds, did seem
To visit me, and me alone;
Me, unapproached by any friend,
Save those who to my sorrows lend
Tears due unto their own.

IV

To-night the church-tower bells will ring
Through these wide realms a festive peal;
To the new year a welcoming;
A tuneful offering for the weal
Of happy millions lulled in sleep;
While I am forced to watch and weep,
By wounds that may not heal.

V

Born all too high, by wedlock raised
Still higher—to be cast thus low!
Would that mine eyes had never gazed
On aught of more ambitious show
Than the sweet flowerets of the fields!
—It is my royal state that yields
This bitterness of woe.

VI

Yet how?—for I, if there be truth
In the world's voice, was passing fair;
And beauty, for confiding youth,
Those shocks of passion can prepare
That kill the bloom before its time;
And blanch, without the owner's crime,
The most resplendent hair.

VII

Unblest distinction! showered on me
To bind a lingering life in chains:
All that could quit my grasp, or flee,
Is gone;—but not the subtle stains
Fixed in the spirit; for even here
Can I be proud that jealous fear
Of what I was remains.

VIII

A Woman rules my prison's key;
A sister Queen, against the bent
Of law and holiest sympathy,
Detains me, doubtful of the event;
Great God, who feel'st for my distress,
My thoughts are all that I possess,
O keep them innocent!

IX

Farewell desire of human aid,
Which abject mortals vainly court!
By friends deceived, by foes betrayed,
Of fears the prey, of hopes the sport;
Nought but the world-redeeming Cross
Is able to supply my loss,
My burthen to support.

X

Hark! the death-note of the year
Sounded by the castle-clock!
From her sunk eyes a stagnant tear
Stole forth, unsettled by the shock;
But oft the woods renewed their green,
Ere the tired head of Scotland's Queen
Reposed upon the block!

WILLIAM WORDSWORTH [1770–1850]

Mary Queen of Scots arrives at Lochleven
where she would be incarcerated for almost a year,
1567–8

'The Song'

'O! Lady dear, fair is thy noon,
But man is like the inconstant moon:
Last night she smiled o'er lawn and lea;
That moon will change, and so will he.

'Thy time, dear Lady, 's a passing shower;
Thy beauty is but a fading flower;
Watch thy young bosom, and maiden eye,
For the shower must fall, and the flow'ret die.'

   What ails my Queen? said good Argyle,
Why fades upon her cheek the smile?
Say, rears your steed too fierce and high?
Or sits your golden seat awry?

. . .

   Queen Mary lighted in the court;
Queen Mary joined the evening's sport;
Yet though at table all were seen,
To wonder at her air and mien;
Though courtiers fawned and ladies sung,
Still in her ear the accents rung; –
'Watch thy young bosom, and maiden eye,
For the shower must fall, and the flow'ret die.'
These words prophetic seemed to be,
Foreboding wo and misery;
And much she wished to prove ere long,
The wonderous powers of Scottish song.

JAMES HOGG [1770–1835]
from *The Queen's Wake*

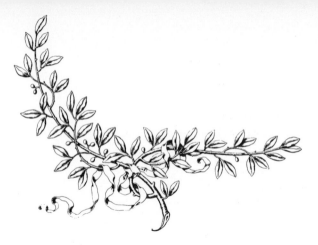

Upon the block she laid her head
She was as calm as if in bed
One of the men her head did hold
And then her head was of I'm told
There ends all Queen Elisbeths foes
And those who at her bend their bows
Elisbeth was a cross old maid
Now when her youth began to fade
Her temper was worce then before
And people did not her adore
But Mary was much loved by all
Both by the great and by the small
But hark her soul to heaven did rise
And I do think she gained a prise
For I do think she would not go
Into the awfull place below
There is a thing that I must tell
Elisbeth went to fire and hell
Him who will teach her to be civel
It must be her great friend the divel.

MARJORY FLEMING [1803–11]

Adieux à Marie Stuart

I

Queen, for whose house my fathers fought,
    With hopes that rose and fell,
Red star of boyhood's fiery thought,
    Farewell.

They gave their lives, and I, my queen,
    Have given you of my life,
Seeing your brave star burn high between
    Men's strife.

The strife that lightened round their spears
    Long since fell still: so long
Hardly may hope to last in years
    My song.

But still through strife of time and thought
    Your light on me too fell:
Queen, in whose name we sang or fought,
    Farewell.

II

There beats no heart on either border
    Wherethrough the north blasts blow
But keeps your memory as a warder
    His beacon-fire aglow.

Long since it fired with love and wonder
　　Mine, for whose April age
Blithe midsummer made banquet under
　　The shade of Hermitage.

Soft sang the burn's blithe notes, that gather
　　Strength to ring true:
And air and trees and sun and heather
　　Remembered you.

Old border ghosts of fight or fairy
　　Or love or teen,
These they forgot, remembering Mary
　　The Queen.

III

Queen once of Scots and ever of ours
　　Whose sires brought forth for you
Their lives to strew your way like flowers,
　　Adieu.

Dead is full many a dead man's name
　　Who died for you this long
Time past: shall this too fare the same,
　　My song?

*The trial of Mary Queen of Scots in a room
above the great hall of Fotheringhay Castle, 15 October 1586*

But surely, though it die or live,
   Your face was worth
All that a man may think to give
   On earth.

No darkness cast of years between
   Can darken you:
Man's love will never bid my queen
   Adieu.

IV

Love hangs like light about your name
   As music round the shell:
No heart can take of you a tame
   Farewell.

Yet, when your very face was seen,
   Ill gifts were yours for giving:
Love gat strange guerdons of my queen
   When living.

O diamond heart unflawed and clear,
   The whole world's crowning jewel!
Was ever heart so deadly dear
   So cruel?

Yet none for you of all that bled
   Grudged once one drop that fell:
Not one to life reluctant said
   Farewell.

V

Strange love they have given you, love disloyal,
   Who mock with praise your name,
To leave a head so rare and royal
   Too low for praise or blame.

You could not love nor hate, they tell us,
    You had nor sense nor sting:
In God's name, then, what plague befell us
    To fight for such a thing?

'Some faults the gods will give', to fetter
    Man's highest intent:
But surely you were something better
    Than innocent!

No maid that strays with steps unwary
    Through snares unseen,
But one to live and die for; Mary,
    The Queen.

VI

Forgive them all their praise, who blot
    Your fame with praise of you:
Then love may say, and falter not,
    Adieu.

Yet some you hardly would forgive
    Who did you much less wrong
Once: but resentment should not live
    Too long.

They never saw your lip's bright bow,
    Your swordbright eyes,
The bluest of heavenly things below
    The skies.

Clear eyes that love's self finds most like
    A swordblade's blue,
A swordblade's ever keen to strike,
    Adieu.

Though all things breathe or sound of fight
   That yet make up your spell,
To bid you were to bid the light
   Farewell.

Farewell the song says only, being
   A star whose race is run:
Farewell the soul says never, seeing
   The sun.

Yet, wellnigh as with flash of tears,
   The song must say but so
That took your praise up twenty years
   Ago.

More bright than stars or moons that vary,
   Sun kindling heaven and hell,
Here, after all these years, Queen Mary,
   Farewell.

ALGERNON CHARLES SWINBURNE [1837–1909]

*Elizabeth suggests to Davison,
the secretary of the Privy Council, that Sir Amyas Paulet
secretly poison Mary, February 1587*

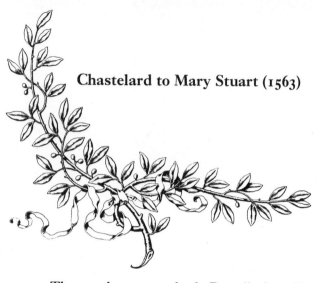

Chastelard to Mary Stuart (1563)

Then send me to my death. But wilt thou rid
Thy life of me thereby? If in the gloom
Of thy adored and silent balmy room
My ghost should glide, where once I parting hid?
At night thou'lt see me; though thou close thy lid
As tightly as they soldered down my tomb,
And feel a kiss—thou shalt know well of whom—
Scorch thee as living kisses never did.
When thou shalt die, at Heaven's gate I'll sit
And watch the stream of silent souls that wend
Through the great arch, till thou approachst it.
Or if thy doom be flame, I shall descend
Through all the caverns where the lost souls flit,
To find and clasp thee at their endless end.

EUGENE LEE-HAMILTON [1845–1907]
from *Imaginary Sonnets*

The Tragic Mary Queen of Scots, II

I could wish to be dead!
Too quick with life were the tears I shed,
Too sweet for tears is the life I led;
And ah, too lonesome my marriage-bed!
I could wish to be dead.

I could wish to be dead,
For just a word that rings in my head;
Too dear, too dear are the words he said,
They must never be rememberèd.
I could wish to be dead.

I could wish to be dead:
The wish to be loved is all mis-read,
And to love, one learns when one is wed,
Is to suffer bitter shame; instead
I could wish to be dead.

'Michael Field' (KATHARINE BRADLEY [1846–1914]
and EDITH COOPER [1862–1913])

Alas! Poor Queen

She was skilled in music and the dance
And the old arts of love
At the court of the poisoned rose
And the perfumed glove,
And gave her beautiful hand
To the pale Dauphin
A triple crown to win—
And she loved little dogs
                And parrots
                        And red-legged partridges
And the golden fishes of the Duc de Guise
And a pigeon with a blue ruff
She had from Monsieur d'Elbœuf.

Master John Knox was no friend to her;
She spoke him soft and kind,
Her honeyed words were Satan's lure
The unwary soul to bind.
'Good sir, doth a lissome shape
And a comely face
Offend your God His Grace
Whose Wisdom maketh these
Golden fishes of the Duc de Guise?'

She rode through Liddesdale with a song;
'Ye streams sae wondrous strang,
Oh, mak' me a wrack as I come back
But spare me as I gang.'
While a hill-bird cried and cried
Like a spirit lost
By the grey storm-wind tost.

Consider the way she had to go,
Think of the hungry snare,
The net she herself had woven,
Aware or unaware,
Of the dancing feet grown still,
The blinded eyes—
Queens should be cold and wise,
And she loved little things,
      Parrots
        And red-legged partridges
And the golden fishes of the Duc de Guise
And the pigeon with the blue ruff
She had from Monsieur d' Elbœuf.

MARION ANGUS [1866–1946]

The execution of Mary Queen of Scots,
8 February 1587, at Fotheringhay

from The Burial of a Queen

They carried her down with singing,
   With singing sweet and low,
Slowly round the curve they came,
Twenty torches dropping flame,
The heralds that were bringing her
   The way we all must go.

'Twas master William Dethik,
   The Garter King of Arms,
Before her royal coach did ride,
With none to see his Coat of Pride,
For peace was on the country-side,
   And sleep upon the farms;

Peace upon the red farm,
   Peace upon the grey,
Peace on the heavy orchard trees,
And little white-walled cottages,
Peace upon the wayside,
   And sleep upon the way.

So Master William Dethik,
   With forty horse and men,
Like any common man and mean
Rode on before the Queen, the Queen,
And—only a wandering pedlar
   Could tell the tale again.

How, like a cloud of darkness,
    Between the torches moved
Four black steeds and a velvet pall
Crowned with the Crown Imperial
And—on her shield—the lilies,
    The lilies that she loved.

Ah, stained and ever stainless,
Ah, white as her own hand,
White as the wonder of that brow,
Crowned with colder lilies now,
White on the velvet darkness,
    The lilies of her land!

The witch from over the water,
    The fay from over the foam,
The bride that rode thro' Edinbro' town
With satin shoes and a silken gown,
A Queen, and a great king's daughter,—
    Thus they carried her home,

With torches and with scutcheons,
    Unhonoured and unseen,
With the lilies of France in the wind a-stir,
And the Lion of Scotland over her,
Darkly, in the dead of night,
    They carried the Queen, the Queen!

ALFRED NOYES [1880–1958]
from *Tales of the Mermaid Tavern*

The Queen of Scotland's Reply
to a Reproof from John Knox

Said the bitter Man of Thorns to me, the White
   Rose-Tree:
'That wonted love of yours is but an ass's bray —
The beast who called to beast
And kicked the world away!'
(All the wisdom of great Solomon
Held in an ass's bray.)

When body to body, soul to soul
Were bare in the fire of night
As body to grave, as spirit to Heaven or Hell,
What did we say?
'Ah, too soon we shall be air —
No pleasure, anguish, will be possible.
Hold back the day!'
For in this moment of the ass-furred night
You called the hour of the Beast, was born
All the wisdom of great Solomon
From the despisèd clay!
All the wisdom of Solomon
Held in an ass's bray.

EDITH SITWELL [1887–1964]

from **Bacchanalia**

Lights converge on the theatre: Zims, Zisses
And Tatras, a pavement-blinding cavalcade.
Lost in the blizzard, black market ticket sellers
Prolong the uselessness of their blockade.

We jostle in to Mary Queen of Scots
Through ranks as close as ranks of halberdiers.
Young people change their vouchers for a ticket
And greet the actress with a blaze of cheers.

*   *   *

Outside the door they're scuffling for a ticket;
From gloom of stage the canvas settings grow.
The Queen of Scots appears, sudden as if
She'd left the dance a minute or two ago.

Her life and liberty pound against her ribs;
Prison can't crack her in its stone duress;
She's born to be restless as a dragonfly,
To capture hearts and hurt with a caress;

And these are the reasons why the fiery queen
Must bow her head to the executioner's hand.
She sits beside a table; a row of footlights
Edges her grey skirt with a brilliant band.

To this coquette, dizzy adventure, Paris,
Ronsard, the stage and verse are all the same,
All nothing. Sentenced, she's careless of food and shelter,
The moated fort and the reflector's flame.

Her death's heroic; this keeps her at her prime,
Wraps her in rumour; she's the talk of time.

*   *   *

A common lust for danger, common joy and pain
Have welded role and actress into one.
Across so many years the turbulent leading lady
Gives the dead queen the chance to slip her chain.

It's a rare courage, and the luck is rare,
To play for the centuries as gullies play
And as the river plays, given no choice,
Like wine and diamonds and the girl whose hair

Was plaited in a bun, who wore a stripe on white
And played for simple people on the opening night.

BORIS PASTERNAK [1890–1960]
Translated by Michael Harari

The translation of Mary's body to Peterborough Cathedral,
30 July 1587, after lying for six months in Fotheringhay

John Knox

That scything wind has cut the rich corn down –
the satin shades of France spin idly by –
the bells are jangled in St Andrew's town –
a thunderous God tolls from a northern sky.
He pulls the clouds like bandages awry.
See how the harlot bleeds below her crown.
This lightning stabs her in the heaving thigh –
such siege is deadly for dallying gown.

A peasant's scythe rings churchbells from the stone.
From this harsh battle let the sweet birds fly,
surprised by fields, now barren of their corn.
(Invent, bright friends, theology, or die.)
The shearing naked absolute blade has torn
through false French roses to her foreign cry.

IAIN CRICHTON SMITH [1928–]

On a Portrait
of Mary Queen of Scots,
in Captivity (1578)

You are looking at a face
Dismissed from Paradise.
Nothing recalls the place.
No-one can hear the cries.

ANTHONY ASTBURY [1940–]

Index
of Poets and Translators